No Accident

Aaron Anstett

Winner of the Backwaters Prize for 2004

The Backwaters Press

First Printing, 800 copies, May 2005

The Backwaters Press
3502 North 52nd Street
Omaha, NE 68104-3506
(402) 451-4052
gkosm62735@aol.com
www.thebackwaterspress.homestead.com

ISBN: 0-9765231-2-4

JUDGE'S STATEMENT

I read a great many poems by young American poets. I've been doing this for over fifty years, since in fact I was a young, unknown American poet out to discover the nature of his competition. That's exactly how I first found the work of Kinnell, Rich, Snyder, Hecht, Levertov, Creeley, Ginsberg, Merwin—many of the best poets of my generation. Their work told me something I needed to hear: I was going to have to become a hell of a lot better writer if I were ever to regard myself as a true poet. Although I may have begun this venture into poetry in an effort to assess my own talent, in the long run what I found was great inspiration, the knowledge that I was part of a generation that had the talent, vision, originality, and determination to add something significant to American poetry.

At seventy-six I'm still reading the young, no longer with the notion of competing, but much more in an effort to discover if these young people speak my language or if I'm up to hearing their language. And also in an effort to put the lie to the often-repeated pseudo-fact that the writing workshops have killed off any individuality and daring in our writers—that's how I found writers as diverse as Jane Mead, Li-Young Lee, Kate Daniels, Tom Sleigh, Rodney Jones, Kathleen Peirce, to name a few. Now I'd like to add to that list of singular poets the name of Aaron Anstett, whose book *No Accident* is unlike any book of American poems I've ever read before. Maybe I love this book so much because Anstett has done something I could never do, would not even dare to try: he's employed some of the tactics of Cesar Vallejo—arguably the finest American poet of the last hundred years and certainly the most furious and experimental—and he's done so without falling under the sway of the great Peruvian and simply imitating him: Vallejo is only one of a number of poetic influences that have come together to form Anstett's uniquely American voice.

Let me also make it clear I find Anstett's poetry in possession of two qualities that for me are essential to the poetry of Vallejo as well as most of the American poetry I admire—humility and compassion—qualities that life and not graduate workshops instill (though workshops do not obliterate them in people of character). But no, Anstett is not our little Vallejo, for he is also in possession of a marvelous and zany sense of humor, which may owe more to the Marx brothers than any poet who comes to mind. He is decidedly North American and of the present, and even with his epic disrespect and cosmic belly laughs he is ultimately a poet of great humanity and hope:

> In the few scraps blown in after the asphalt was swept
> and the pyramid of mortared cannonballs in the park off the
> highway,
>
> where the swings hang absolutely still, as if painted there, we find
> our joy always.
> And there, on the photograph's left edge, the birds eternally
> arriving.

(from "Afterlife")

That's not Vallejo or Kenneth Koch or James Tate, That's something entirely unexpected and original from a powerful imagination like no other. Aaron Anstett's *No Accident* is here for anyone who needs to replenish the belief that American poetry is as healthy and useful as it ever was.

Philip Levine, July 2004

One

"Rejoice, orphan; down your shot of water
from the general store on any corner."

—Cesar Vallejo

AFTERLIFE

Perhaps the four-color photograph of a lube stop and car wash,
like a heaven above the numbered days and months of a giveaway
      calendar,

is heaven and shall be our dominion forever, with glare on the glass
      doors
and lettering spelling something. Maybe the man with
      indistinguishable features

standing on a sidewalk runs things, and those driving vehicles
      somewhere
for eternity: heaven's emissaries, the interrupting angels, who veer

from this to that world. In the few scraps blown in after the asphalt
      was swept
and the pyramid of mortared cannonballs in the park off the
      highway,

where the swings hang absolutely still, as if painted there, we find our
      joy always.
And there, on the photograph's left edge, the birds eternally arriving.

EXACTITUDE

A residential hotel burns,
fire, in varying colors and amounts,
walking the duplicate rooms.
Who, without distance, would be such a stickler?
Who, not dying, could discern primary from hue?

All we can prove, the fire's a uniform, gas-stove blue.
Say there are casualties, one or two.
Smoke, the better angels of our natures hope,
took them more deeply into unconsciousness.
Consider the problem of plural views.

Inhabitants, if they stayed long
or supposed they would, have hung pin-ups
and crucifixes, rearranged the repeated furniture,
so the scenes, even shared, can only ever be similar.
Flames on closed curtains let no view through.

Turn from the burning to any metaphor.
Like fire, it eventually equates everything,
believes the fire human because fire is not inanimate.
We say fire eavesdrops and fire is a transient,
and we claim fire's aspects: rage and a relative brevity.

Already I've forgotten the people.
Some sleep on. Some rise and run.
Like me, you mostly do not know them. Like me,
you are as unable as them or the bright wallpaper
to say exactly what any of this is or stop it.

HISTORY

No one in this world remembers making love in 1648,
though somebody must have, maybe everyone did,

or recalls the exact angle to which a sparrow bent a pine branch
        afterwards,
shaking loose a little rain nestled in the needles there,

or can say with any certainty what that sounded like,
whether breath, or skin against skin, or nothing.

MANIFEST

> "Man, I been thirsty."
> —John Berryman

One glass of water, the universal solvent,
has, in all its manifest elements, suffered

all things atmospheric. It makes a drinker simple.
The captive liquid, part tumultuary

as a fevered, stringhalt horse,
part insensate as an arctic carcass,

is three states of matter incarnate.
It has risen and fallen and lain still in ditches.

Even blurry, it's vivid.
In the janitor's veins or bucket,

in the dictator's tears and the widow's bath,
water bears no lasting traces.

It ought to be inconsolable. Drink, then.
Existence means complicity with terrible necessities.

DRINKS

In taverns named for dire conditions,
On a Bender, Eighty-Sixed, Thirsty Sharks,

Jackson sat long and drank from dawn to dark.
Night monotoned the standard rendition:

slow to quick drinks, brief grace to perdition.
Day starts with bird song, ends in dog barks.

Who sleeps well tonight in public parks?
Jackson awoke in awkward positions:

doorways, cocaine traced across cracked, glass plates,
week's pay, rain-wet; someone's shower stall;

who's-its porch swing; what criminal's couch?
Names on newsprint caught in sewer grates

stay names. The orbits survive us all,
and that bad tosspot Jackson's head hurts. Ouch.

That bad tosspot Jackson's head hurts. Ouch.
Light pours all over him. He cannot last.

His face his father's, the sun a real bastard,
Jackson believes he's what rough beast slouches

toward Bethlehem. Watch, watch, watch, watch, watch:
he walks by the mirroring storefronts fast,

avoids his own eyes, little fright mask
stuck on the skull in which his wet brain's sloshed.

Get this man some vivid, strong liquor quick.
Too bad he's spent his literal last cent

this morning on a pack of cigarettes.
He lights one with a tavern match and flicks

it out. Go find it on that sidewalk, bent
by Jackson's fingers, alive, though he forgets.

*

Jackson's fingers (alive, though he forgets)
touched everything he touched: dying hands,

newborns, miles of skin, tossed contraband,
acres of pages, dirt, milk-swollen breasts,

but these they cradle and remember best:
beer cans, bottles, their lids and glass, the strand

of printed paper on the whisky's cap and
maker's labeled promise and forced health threats.

Jackson's poured vodka into paper cups
with a little vermouth and served himself.

He's used his own fingers to mix a drink.
They don't shake. Sobriety interrupts

him often. He's still as a coastal shelf.
Jackson's OK. He's functioning. He thinks.

Jackson's OK. He's functioning. He thinks,
"Sunrise over China. Great God above.

The grand plant life alcohol is made of
circumscribes the world, its blossom and stink

rich in the villages where small birds blink,
and large birds, and none. Those flowers and fluff:

ancestors set some out to rot and loved
what happened: dizzying liquid that links,

it seems, man to God, Jackson to bigger
being. This wash washes all, erases

last night's mistakes, bathes tomorrow's sorrows.
Pain in the world is too much to figure.

Who first? Which town? What evidence, traces
of crushing ancestry, grief Jackson knows?"

Of crushing, ancestral grief, Jackson knows
this much: too much. He'd rather tie one on.

That's why bars open early, the reason
neon's lit in daylight, how money goes

so swiftly, and why the many zeroes
of bottles' mouths yawn on until stark dawn.

Jackson drinks at each drink until it's gone,
orders more, drinks until the swollen scene shows

through his magnifying glass: fast bar clock,
dimmed and brightened faces, shelved bottles lined

in drunken alphabetical order.
Patsy Cline plays on every jukebox

he can think of. Jackson asks the closed blinds,
"Ever have a morning eye-opener?"

*

"Ever have a morning eye-opener,"
asks Jackson, "lose a day, suffer blackouts?"

Ever cower while a woman shouts
at another through the locked apartment door

and calls your name and calls you a liar
or walk heel-toe as a policeman doubts

you're sober? Ever rummage for and count
each coin in the house then go buy liquor?

Hard to stack them drunk. Hard to come up short
at a counter and argue with the clerk

you'll bring the rest by soon. Ever see men
ask for one free one from the gleaming quart

they stare at instead of the man at work
behind the bar? They know it won't happen.

*

Behind the bar, they know it won't happen:
drinks pouring themselves, humorous phrases

carved in wood pointing a way, their faces
suddenly those on currency or thin

and young in the mirror. Light won't begin
shining from their eyes, lighting the places

they look and illuminating graces
each thought the others lost. Still, they drink in

drink on drink as if something were revealed.
It seems what is seen there cannot be told

until one begs one more drink's permission.
It seems drink by drink alone is healed.

We drink them. We order and grow old
in taverns named for dire conditions.

GOOD MORNING

Fifty-some years after the war, a kamikaze lands in my yard,
gently, like a sheet of newsprint.

"Ohayo gozaimasu," I say, though it is evening, light grown ochre
and pink, day disappearing across the Zero's wings.

He shinnies from the cockpit, the thinnest man I've seen.
He has evaded the radar. He's fallen

for decades, believing he'll attack
the coast of America, setting all the pines in Oregon blazing.

I take him inside, where he drinks a glass of water.
It is clear. It tastes nothing like the ocean.

GOD'S JOB

I surface in an office,
answering phones under false name. To keep from sleeping,

I wear contact lenses of transparent pornographic photographs
so I see my coworkers in the light of minglings,

as if they floated in a palimpsest of their first history.
For fear of being pink-slipped, I do not exclaim, "No wonder.

They're someone's pleasure and someone's suffering."
In one pocket: a miniature of this city. In the other: a brick.

I alphabetize the file drawers labeled *Desires* and *Fears*.
The false name? I'm sworn to secrecy.

MATTER

Matter goes by its many aliases: pine tree, match stick, missile
     whistling
increasingly distant from its silo and signal. All over America,

someone puts 40 cents of gasoline into a 15-year-old car, has beer
     and peanut butter,
sleeps in an arm chair outside her room in a work release motel north
     of town,

wakes on heating grates, wonders how the flower knows what shape
     to take,
watches the scrambled pornographic channel, prays hard. Only,
     scattered

on the land, fire, that natural redhead, is and acts, undoes the field
     mice
and grasses, makes the old book's pages frailer. We must turn them
     carefully.

IF I HAD ANOTHER FACE

"If I had another face, do you think I would wear this one?"
—Lincoln-Douglas Debates

"Abe Lincoln Was the Father of Professional Wrestling!"
—*Weekly World News*

1.
Once, as a young man, Abe Lincoln choked on a cherry stone.
His eyes grew bigger. His face turned colors.
Abe Lincoln clutched his own throat, tilted over the dropped axe
whose handle pointed to the stand of trees
where the wood he'd been splitting bloomed.
A crow crossed over. It was noon.

2
Abe Lincoln chortles at the joke he's told
to the mother of a boy who's died in the war
come two days by horse to visit him.
He touches his forehead, catches his breath,
repeats the punch line, "A fly in the butter churn. A fly."

3.
Leaves pitch in a fit of wind.
It's uncommonly sunny.
Some rise from piles.
Some just now falling are caught in the currents.
Abe Lincoln watches them.
They will not arrange themselves this way again.

4.
A masked Abe Lincoln prowls the ring.

GRAMMAR

As if no language existed beyond that transmitted via drive-through
     window speakers
and we were forced to build from these few words the names of
     items for purchase

and their prices a lexicon and grammar capable of conveyance so
     conjuring
pity, fright, and longing ensued in listeners, yet so clear one could
     warn

of open manholes and rabid, racing animals, all purposes served,
     communication
largely a matter of context, duration, and inflection, in what setting
     and pauses

and stresses where transforming, "Can I get you anything else today"
     from "I envy
you your good fortune" to "This conversation has grown
     wearisome,"

"Here's your drinks" from "Not a cloud" to "Cancer," cents and
     dollars
Dewey-decimaled, so one amount refers to body parts, another to a
     movie star,

I mean it when I say, "Have a nice day. Drive on through. What kind
     of sauce?"
Say I name my moods, as if I might thus tame them, assign them
     codes like chess moves,

call the one I'm in "Dusk Sky over Berlin," "Stampede" the one I'm
    slouching to,
"Deliverance of the Angels" when I kiss you, when we bicker
    "Shooter on the Roof,"

with my weird Eden Adamed, indexed, might I then whistle my
    moods home
like animals, call their names and be stricken with them, pills that take
    hold

when commanded and always give; wasn't it this way for the first
    man: all phenomena
passed-out flesh some color returns to when called by the most
    plausible sounds,

yet left a little diminished, steaming water after frost-bite, worst cure
long-term, but the first, most comforting thought, or did the words
    aggrandize,

make more of the much and little already there, or even slow and
    lukewarm
water, did they restore, return, as only you can, sensation in its
    terrifying measures?

AND THEN

Often I'm afraid a missile an anvil a bank safe will descend

pow on my head smackdab on the bald spot right through the circle
  it's said

the chakra the soul ascends and sets out on its rounds then my brain
  pan

soft pallet undoing all those dentists' labor shuttling through my
  thorax

and torso stomach splashing last night's wine and hummus

It happens in cities New York Chicago plummeting scaffolding and
  cornices

Or my sad-sack dumb fuck cousin last I saw him small boy

at the funeral just before that the deathbed making fish lips like our
  grandfather's

dentureless gasping mouth then smacked in the face by my uncle

his father who saw me scowl then 21 two months out of prison
  breaking

and entering he claimed innocence of on the West side buying drugs

just smoke his friend in the car told police led down an alley and then

ALIAS

I'm the state enemy absent in the photographs
employees retouch, replaced with scenery:
extra steps to the lectern

where the famous mouth holds forth, the feared arms
gesture, the reproduction oil painting
in my children's children's classrooms.

I'm the quality of light expunged from lenses,
face that never struck a retina
through glass, altering a film of chemicals.

I'm the one on coins and stamps
if a currency commemorates the shadow
and the potted plant, in that country where a park's

named for me: *Slit With Razors From the Negatives,*
and in that park the statue honoring me
stands life-size: the censor's expert hands.

EVERY STEP A TRESPASS

Our bodies must,
it seems, be beaten
by police or made to work
for so much an hour.

The unlikely hands, the vacant,
impossible mouths, susceptible as air
to mayhem in daylight, make small
crime sites, localize grief.

We grow untenable,
edge toward anonymity, as if languidly
waking or the space a mouth makes
crossing every inch of us

never once occurred, even
in yearning. Corpses don't opt,
mine, or yours, or the bird's
my daughter broke my grasp

today to hold and lift
up high above the grass. Scolding
and scolding her, I washed her hands raw.
Buried, we cast no shade. We're bare as all outdoors.

SHANTY

Shame I can't treasure my skeleton,
prop it and toss glitter on it,
lift it and dance around with it.

Shucks that I can't show it off,
each bone there's a name for,
my expensive acquisition.

I'd pose it in positions,
Washington crossing the Delaware,
Mussolini head-tilt,

with scraps of newsprint in the eye sockets
and rags in the cranium.
A red paper heart to hang in the rib cage.

Gosh-darn that I can't see it outside of me,
my lily-white hinges, ankles
and scary bare knuckles.

I'd hoist it off the front porch
in high winds, unnerve
neighbors when it clatters.

MY SENTIMENTAL EDUCATION

Who poked Bazooka Joe's lost eye, what jape
was his gang engaged in, what joke
gone wrong, involving explosives

beer bottles were stolen
from their sleeping fathers for?
Maybe Bazooka caught a rusty nail

looking under the rug to see the floor show.
Maybe he stared and stared
through the wrong keyhole.

We'll never know. They never say
what happened to Joe. The eye patch is given.
All else is joking. Such lives,

they have to laugh though, and hard,
knocked twenty degrees backwards
a foot off the ground

every punch line, stunned into shooting
lines out their heads, black lines that float
like flattened haloes. It's a means of survival

for Bazooka and his gang, being poor, but proud,
with one set of clothes. Bazooka's always grinning
in his blue ball cap. Bazooka's always dumbfounding

the adults into stupor, and so never has to
go to sleep, mismatched pajamas and dirty sheets,
yanking the knotted shoelace down,

then walk across his small room so
tiptoed his ankles hurt, lying there in bed just
a skinny kid with one eye gone.

CLEANING

That's my face gaping in the hygienist's goggles, extra-simian,
eyes wide as a lab animal's, my mouth's blood on her surgical gloves.
She's all business, grim.

She scrapes the part of me most skeletal
so fiercely with instruments my ribs flinch.
It's all negligence and damage where those tiny harpoons land,

but who knew nerve ends meant this
blatancy, this weird, shimmery flutter in the chest?
Horizontal in the chair, I could be an autopsy,

may already occupy the fabled grave, except I see her,
my tongue all thumbs on the back of the mirror, and hear
country-and-western Muzak meant to soothe, or maybe that's the
        proof

I'm out of body, headed some worse earth.
In the window above the dentist's stuffed bass, a hairy wrist
wipes a wet rag. The head that governs it looks in at me and grins.

BARLEY

Soon I'll zoom through the hoop of your arms
and plant a smacker, let my heels drift,
pivot where each twin lip lumbers
to a long and longer kiss, like animals up an ark.

Tie a-dangle, I'll float
all Chagall above the waist above you.
I'll see down your blousy, yellow dress.

The space between our faces is a shrinking peasant village.
The crop this year is barley.
My eyes are the butchers.
Your two are the rabbis.

AUGURY

When was it it seemed earth would give way underfoot,
where we trembled all over each other's x-y coordinates, acrobatic

in a kitchen, party roiling in the living room, conga line
of bare-chested men fabricating Spanish oaths and expletives,
        jumping

so the walls shook, rolling *r*'s in the brightening dark, in which birds
        woke,
practiced their racket, as, suddenly upstairs, we mastered every
        manner

of quackery quickly, skins' salts alchemical, you basing grave cautions
on my rib cage's curves, "An early grave; fear thunder and water,"

me granting long life by tracing across you the lower- and upper-case
alphabets, first standard script, then cursive, in long, halting
        sentences?

$500,000 POLICY

Spend every cent on my final expenses:
fireworks and rock bands, one fur-lined coffin

for each card in my wallet, truckloads of snacks:
nacho chips and Chuckles, your Ring Dings and Corn Nuts.

Tattoo labels on my eyelids, one per:
Never Better or *Miss You*. Outline the skeleton

along my skin with black-light ink, Latin names
in cursive script. Finance a student film

of my libretto, contralto, from beyond the grave,
beyond the range of human hearing, twenty-four hours

of "Race car, race car, race car" backwards fast.
Fly a TV-special magician and whatever assistants

right here. Hire them at any cost to cut me in half
for real and make those pieces disappear.

WHAT PROFITS A MAN

My press-on stigmata wow you more than my prescience,
re: where the face of Jesus will surface next: bearded and grinning
on each tortilla hand-flattened by Mrs. R. of Austin, Texas,
then fried in the fat that sketches and fills in his features,

every one a replica, so we mail-order and eat them, heated,
or so sorrowful and pained in the plate-glass smudges reappearing
next morning, no matter what cleaner, at the Alhambra Discount
        Theater,
address undisclosed, but near the ticket window, as the movie credits

roll, slow, and their letters rearrange, spell prayers and verses
ticket-holders utter. Watch for helicopters, television coverage,
box office boom. A woman sleeping with her children under
        cardboard
and an asphalt bridge awakes in leaky rain. Her looking makes a
        mirror

of a puddle and her eyes grow suddenly blue and bigger, like the
        paintings.
"God damn," she says, "God damn, God damn, God damn."
Her name's Arlene. Just ask her. The weeks-old sheets
of newsprint animated by a wind, their photographs now moving
        pictures,

broadcast a film on fences: documents the president secretly signed,
who the mayor had killed, which knife your neighbor
held to her throat, what all the children ate. There's my ad: Press-On
        Stigmata,
4 for $10. I seem to be bleeding. I drip. My wounds look convincing.

Two

"The little hole in the eye
Williams called it, the little hole

Has exposed us naked
To the world

And will not close."

—George Oppen

SCENES

Against the lingerie-color sunset,

orange and pink and filmy as a negligee, two dogs
fight in a liquor store parking lot, mouths on
throats, blood an inkling in the neon advertising
bargains on imports. Their long shadows go slo-
mo in the skittering gravel and spin under dust's
little weather systems. Customers seem to glow,
sidling past then leaving with purchases.

woozily in a room the knockout gas has seeped through, making the rug and the lampshade and the couch smell like medicine. A man whistles and tilts, does a dance called "My Whole Body Feels Like an Arm I've Slept Funny On." He believes he's an iceberg. He thinks he's a thundercloud. Suddenly he sings, "Oh, I could die right here, in the delirium of air."

Footprints in a prison yard's snow,

different sizes of the same shoe in loopy, raggedy patterns, fill with those drifting hieroglyphs falling a long way to shine all night in the floodlights. They scroll in horizontal lines like a stream of arbitrary numbers. Snow fills the nest a bird has built bit by bit by bit (burnt matches, newsprint, hair) in the fence's concertina wire.

the basement boiler seen past them looks
shimmery catch fire. How leisurely flames stroll
unfinished wallboards. Through attic windows,
angled daylight, speckled with dust, shines on a
dictionary with pages stained yellow, orange, and
purple with pressed summer wildflowers.

The antique pornographic film

projected across a kneeling man's unclothed back,
bodies doing what along his spine, stays nothing
more than light that might well ceaselessly travel,
swift and immaterial, when he rises and steps
aside, but here someone's sudden, outstretched
palm lifts in front of the rays: two torsos splayed
out on the fingers and sepia splashing gallery
walls.

Who is it holds film

up to sunlight beside a parked car in a desert, squinting through each frame threaded between her thumb and forefinger? The engine ticks, and a few lizards flit from cactus to cactus, making time seem to stutter. She stands in a long, flowered dress, seeing far purple hills with one eye and something that makes the expression on her face change and change and change with the other.

Dusk, shadows

grown long on the freshly cut public park grasses,
the few children not called home yet run faster
from swings to slides and back again. The many-
colored lights of televisions sparkle through house
windows all around. One small boy hears his
mother then lies down and plays dead, level with
the lit horizon and bigger than the distant,
scribbled mountains.

Ceiling fans burn

drinkers' cigarettes quicker, adrift in ashtrays, held dreaming between fingers, pressed trembling to lips. One woman shakes hers toward her listener, punctuating points she makes, their faces softened in the long, wavery mirror. One hour, the drink special's over, but who can tell the time in here? The clock between two vodka bottles runs, what, 15, 20, 30 minutes faster?

Noon, a woman

walks from her front door to the mountains, through foothills, where trees run to scrub, then, higher, to aspen. Air thins, and she stops to rest, imagining the purely skeletal repeated figure journeying in scrolls: one person at separate times and increased heights. She stands near a pool of water at the summit in barely enough light to see the house she's traveled far from.

A man puts his hands

on his wife's face as they sleep. She presses her
wrist to the back of his neck. All night they coil
and wreathe like the letters of the alphabet of a
language whose last native speaker died long ago,
their blankets, kicked away and pulled back again,
writing and erasing them. After the alarm clock,
she moves to say something. He puts a finger to
her lips.

Hair waving like lake grasses

fish flicker through—a body standing upright under water seems a body in a larger, larger room—arms held up and forward like a sleepwalker's, who leaves the house in nightclothes to drift through a meadow, head tilted skyward as if searching a ceiling for cracks. Wound around the legs, rope's woven through the cinder blocks it takes to anchor this one, who sways like someone hearing distant, beautiful music.

The body,

surface area inches above the water's, rises and slides over the lip of a claw-footed bathtub, around which floorboards, beneath their checkerboard linoleum, weaken and leak. Single drops spatter a bare carpet downstairs. The body's fall shakes a few photographs from a table. They, too, climb, a few, like the body, face up. On the water's level, ascending finish, the letters of an inked note run.

The tattooist's tattooed hands,

in increasingly ink-splotched surgical gloves, lift
from and lie on a man's stripped chest. When they
lift for the last time: a heart directly above and
same size as the real one, pierced with an arrow
from whose point three tattooed blood-drops drip
blood, all wrapped in a banner lettered with a
woman's name, despite the warning.

Buildings, people,

street-level neon gleam in the moving mirror a
bus window makes in a sunlit city. How much
eyes must see in each filmed frame: drinkers
through a bar's open doorway, one shoe on a
sidewalk, scattering pigeons, and they beaks,
heads, fat bodies lifted on oily wings. *Checks
Cashed, Bail Bonds, Good Food, Tattoo* flash, letters
backwards, across a passenger's sleeping face.

Three

"…the danger that carries us like a mother."

—Denis Johnson

GULF COAST

"Heck," I said, hallucinogenic in Texas City, Texas,
a whistle stop like many days without sleep, the vapory, striated air

combustible and wobbly, the sheen of refined fuel dizzying.
God knows what awfulness-on-the-earth all-told

the colossal, flaring lean-tos on the edge of town were home to.
We ate fried oysters and cole slaw. Our glasses of beer stood yay tall.

Passersby in the windowpane wore expressions
like those on the faces in abnormal psychology texts,

eyes blackened for anonymity but not reprieve from their distress.
They walked around as if undressed.

We sat undermined by substances. The tape loop of my blood
spun. I saw through my closed eyelids

afterimages of Heimlich charts, opened them and read
a government-issue poster: *WHAT TO DO IN CASE OF
        CHEMICAL*

interrupted by her pale, halter-topped bare shoulder,
in which I more sensed than saw the entourage of atoms

shimmying on their hinges. Some outsized cloud of toxic gases
any moment might have risen like a drastic jellyfish.

I said, "Heck." We paid the bill and took our chances. Many
        ambulances
hurried through the sun's last, almost acrobatic light. At the motel,

atoms did their rope tricks. Hands and knees in the bathroom, eyes
inches from the tile, I whispered, "Look here."

LAY MY BURDEN DOWN

Anstett, scofflaw, drives valid licenseless
through the rural *mise-en-scène,* sun
relentless at the extremity of its sweep.

With encyclopedic command of penny-ante illegality,
Anstett, criminally jockeying his standard transmission
one mile an hour under posted limits,

goes uncaught, to and from his latest stint.
Oh, he rakes it in in the world's perpetual elegy
for each prior instant. Anstett has convictions

it all ends in tears. Ask him as he jaunts hungover by
a cow struggling to stand on sheet ice in a pasture,
legs ridiculously splayed and stunningly unperpendicular.

He knows where the damage that used to be animals
has been done by all things vehicular.
When he gets to work, he starts drafting memoranda.

What does Anstett wear
through all this illicitness, motion, and grief?
Wingtips, shirt, and tie. Fridays office casual.

LIFE AND DEATH AT THE DMV

What auspice is this, face crazed
in the photograph I take everywhere as evidence

I'm allowed, bearing the exact expression I'll wear
pulled over for something serious, negligence

laws'll be invented for? I'm one insolent
expletive, all appearances, one dangerous motorist.

I'm driving down the sidewalk backwards drunk,
raising livestock within city limits in the duct-taped trunk,

negotiating turns while reading pornography,
watching the wounded grow small and smaller in front of me.

WORK

Orange trees swayed. A family ate sandwiches
wrapped in newspaper they did not know one word of.
The father scolded the smallest daughter
to put her shirt on, though her breasts had not yet begun.
He hated the mark on her shoulder where the burlap bag had hung.

DECLARATIVE

Some children have caught a small animal.
Birds move jerkily, like early motion photography.
We wait down-river, as if for a child in swathing.
She takes a hallucinogen and sees people pursued by skeletons.
Her canvases come to resemble slaughterhouse workers' clothing.

A man boards a bus with a torso in his carry-on.
The television news anchor's wrists are tied with coat hangers.
The formula spans several chalkboards and carries tremendous
        implications.
Something has made the swans ill; they vomit by the rowboats.
A scuffle on the barge draws a crowd.

Explosive devices lie dormant in the emptied building.
The clock's glass face grows hairline fractures.
A man in the town square talks loudly.
A woman quickly gathers her belongings.
The shop owner unlocks the door.

STORY PROBLEMS

1.
Character X resurfaces in the novel's every chapter,
as if through each of the orange's centrifugal sections,
a book whose pages turn faster and faster.

2.
Character Y wonders which mix of plosives and fricatives
God really hears, and who that is.

3.
We know little about character Z, but she's about to be shot.
Save her by calculating the bullet's trajectory.

HOLES IN THE STORY

1.
If physics allowed actual cartoon thought balloons,
you'd see I'm again daydreaming of miniature hot air balloons
adrift about living rooms and I you
heroin smuggled in stomachs
whose acids dissolve rubber and poison balloons
bloodstreams, souls ascending from bodies like balloons.

2.
Like souls in bodies, air inside balloons remains invisible,
film not yet rinsed in chemicals.
Our ancestors' spidery handwriting grows invisible
on frail and frailer pages going see-through.

3.
Sometimes foreseeing blurry, weeping faces,
I grimace in mirrors for practice,
sober and stoic in those merciless surfaces
like a man I might be one day, who faces
hard news with courage while all around him faces
go watery and he sees souls flicker in voices, faces.

SATELLITES

That's us in the satellite photographs,
in flagrante delicto through the atmosphere.

You can tell by the tattoos: starfish ashore on your ankle,
daggered Ace of Spades bloodless on my shoulder blade.

You're pressing your knuckles to my vestigial tailbone.
I'm saying something urgent to your jugular vein.

See: that pile's what we wore that day: your mismatched lingerie,
my NASA boxer shorts and T-shirt with wine stains.

It seems, at least, we've bathed, but the soles of my feet
shine with calluses. Your toenail polish has flaked.

Thank gravy we're not wearing outfits, or, heavens,
playing Prison Escape. By the sunlight on our bodies,

it's neither early nor late. Something shadows my face.
Your eyes are closed. You've made a cradle of your legs.

POEM FOR A PUBLIC BUS PLACARD

Light changing on passengers' faces,
blank or in conversation, shadowing this then that
skin, my friends, comes far, no matter what language
mouths make or weather reports are broadcast.

Slow motion, flowers fill a yard.
Photographed or no, blood cells plume in marrow.
These here and here are fingerprints. They themselves are innocent.
You clutch the strap and stand. I see your heart beat in your wrist.

EMPIRE

A day so slow it might be medicated,
and, indeed, we feel chemical in it, dull and glistening,
as if bathed in eye dilator and amber, or wearing

specially alloyed suits beneath our skins, one
per nerve end, so that every gesture's regalia
and erasure, and the simplest utterances, "Flotilla

disappearing," or, "I'm making a loud noise now,"
misheard into import, run rampant.
The present spreads leisurely as pasturage

full of objects nearly quivering, tractors
struggling to approximate themselves, in the slack
and meager glare, in the chronic air.

ZAP

"Zap, zap," some ray-guns say to rag-color pigeons
pecking cement, now dishwater-color smoke and ash.

"Yardbird, yardbird," a short man shouts, with too many clothes on,
slopping vodka, daylight, down his robot throat-hole.

Walk/Don't Walk's the small haiku cross-lights implore.
The dangling window washer, off-season aerialist,

causes little storms each lift of the squeegee
from his red, sudsy bucket. The board he sits on drifts.

LABOR READY/SMOKER FRIENDLY signs insist and *PAID
        TODAY/
CHECKS CASHED HERE.* Meantime, the sun shines

on all these wrist watches. Who shot the pigeons?
What is the proper way for a man to live?

FLESH

A woman's found dead, sun
through the cage of her ribs, wind
at black plastic bags, like rain
in trees. She's half-sunk in earth,
that half earth, half-mirrored in water.
She lies elemental beneath the simple, shifting sky.

One idea of heaven has it squarely in the sky,
without end of bright and clear and calming sun.
There, a spectral music runs like water
and is to adoration as is invisibility to wind.
Here, flesh exists as the spirit's description, sketchy rain
that illustrates falling by falling to earth.

Every animal makes its bargain with the earth.
The woman and her killer share the sky.
Only one of them walks upright in the rain.
On the living and the dead, the sun
shines equally, ancient story, like the wind.
We live and grieve fiercely, mostly water.

Our blood, for its color, tastes of seawater
and its million hidden murders. The earth,
matter, is mostly absence, speckled wind.
Tell that to the gathered family, sky
about the grave site an indifference sun
cannot intend on their despair. A pathetic rain

falls elsewhere. The uncaught killer ambles, rain
no hindrance to his intent. He'll bathe in hot, hot water
that washes over him like sun
across the wicked earth.
His eyes the clean, clear color of sky,
an anger's in him as ungoverned as the wind.

Little, once, a wind
blew rain
sideways in the sky
and knocked her to some water
gathered in the earth.
Next day, her pinned clothes stiffened in the sun.

We struggle and sputter, rain in wind.
We're water falling a long way to earth.
We live a while beneath the sky and sun.

WINTER

At closing time in Davenport, two women kissed fiercely,
as if making some refusal in the terrifying light

suddenly cast across all our faces
and tabletops and plastic cups

of various quantities and conditions of liquid
the law allowed us little time to finish drinking.

I didn't have to go home, but I couldn't stay there.
Bars were still serving across the river.

I read all the notices against fighting and bad checks
and an article about the regular beaten to death

taped to a mirror bearing the bar's name and logo.
Bottles doubled there in image but not content,

then the women, pressed against each other's jackets.
Each had her eyes closed. I cannot know

what it was for them their mouths meant.
One held the other's head as if to steady it.

STRICKEN

Undressed to a skeleton, the curvature mirrored,
shaped like grasses, and stones, and branches,
but worn one color.

The great lengths the wind goes to rustle an orchard,
swerve, and set out elsewhere.

The anvils in my ears stricken.

Sound, like sight, a kind of fiction: narrative travels
and the brain gives refuge.

For all the senses, we make inside us correspondences,
each nerve end an answering chorus.

So the bullet is not substance but sensation.

The hole it opens not absence but displacement.

And saying this will not mend it.

HEAVINESS

> "Heaviness fell into things that had no weight."
> —Ovid

What plunging, where all things quiver and fix.

Still, we feel something inside ourselves drift.

So that we're held on what moving palm, in which fist?

As every stripe of light and air lists.

What seizing, what sense of impending, just before then, then then.

And not the least fallen sparrow goes missed.

PRAYER AGAINST DYING ON CAMERA

Lord, not shot in liquor store stick-up,
jugular uncorked and finely misting or

splatter-patterning display case plate glass
and me so many pixels collapsing

at the feet of bikini'd cardboard
cutout models, purchase a puddle,

last words of my kind, "Oh, shit,"
lip-readable. Jesus not suddenly

in latex novelty emporium or slam-
bang stroke on jumbotron in a coliseum

screaming, not tumbling
from the burning building in a series

of photographs, speed increasing,
one frame famous because I look so calm.

PRAYER FOR SAFE TRAVEL

God bless cars with red cellophane tape over brake lights,
padlocks for trunk locks, different color doors, lumber for bumpers,

windshields zigzag fractals those who outlive lightning wear
everywhere under skin, nearly insignia, tributary maps.

Keep them distant from auto impound's concertina wire,
corkscrewed as cartoon pigs' tails or paper streamers from exploding

party favors. Leave their drivers untroubled. When we follow
open-frame trucks with several green, missile-size bottles

upright and wobbling, extinguish our cigarettes, dispel all fear
and static electricity. Let us clearly see the diamond-shaped
            flammable

symbol, its twist of white lines a burning-bush flicker, its number
3 religious, as promise to spare us while climbing

hills behind dump trucks of jostling rubble and rebar
or vehicle carriers stacked with those spectacular wrecks.

PASTORAL

1.
Murdered girl, man dragged to death through the dirt.

2
Plastic bag tattering the branches of an ordinary tree.

3.
River near which the maples age, darken and brighten and increase
     their rings.

4.
That will not be wholly remembered: kickball game's score in the
     school yard.

5.
Roofs of the train cars flashing like water.

6.
Consider also the little architecture of the mouse's skull.

7.
Daylight's astronomies of insects.

8.
Brightly colored tickets, iced drinks.

9.
Elsewhere.

10.
Here, tinned beans.

11.
The target-practice, buckshot stove.

12.
Someone's ID, someone's set of false teeth.

13.
Face that needs shaving.

14.
Face darkening in the sun.

ARDOR

When I've traveled somewhere so distant I cannot help her,
my very hands buried, or lost, or ash,
when I've come to the world no one returns from,
may my daughter have grown yet more brave and whip-smart

in this one, tall and mouthy, even, eyes far-flung
and beguiling. I would bestow on her the power
to hypnotize landlords and bosses, thugs and policemen,
to pay for all purchases with her singular smile

and return grief to its source. Failing that, I wish her routine
troubles only. Sweet Jesus, nothing outlandish:
her parents' deaths before hers as she approaches her dotage,
one toothache for practice, one flat tire for measure.

May her exaltations be often. May she love whom she loves
with ferocity and hate what she does with equal ardor.
May she believe what I once believed, but longer,
each minute a kingdom, and she the strongest vying sovereign.

ANSWER

For which you'll study the debris-strewn intersections
and stricken faces your remaining days, may they lengthen,
as if some grain of disaster still hovered there,

and you, having isolated it, work at an antidote.
Guesses you hazard: capsule of powdered glass, treatment plan
by which squad lights widen irises, and everything seen

through them thereafter shines. In this shimmer,
you develop your theorem of a fixed measure
of suffering, that there is now no more or less torment

than was or will be, but it wanders. Here a woman
is hurt with pliers. Here the killer watches a comedy.
You call it *No Accident*, and it sustains you,

even thrown through a windshield, stones in your mouth,
even when you drift, combing each tatter of newsprint for what?
Winning numbers? The blazing script of your own name?

You glimpse it in footprints, whatever direction, in road signs
and outdoor advertisements, especially in the eyes of animals
frightened at night: the startling liquid that washes us

ceaselessly, grasses springing back at each step.
Something, you know, is not forthcoming. Something,
like God, is everywhere but hidden, like skin under clothes.

ACKNOWLEDGEMENTS

Grateful acknowledgement is made to the editors of the following magazines in which some of these poems first appeared, sometimes in slightly different versions.

American Letters & Commentary: "History"
Artful Dodge: "Cleaning," "Matter"
Black Warrior Review: "Answer"
The Blue Moon Review: "Lay My Burden Down"
Copper Nickel: "Holes in the Story"
The Eleventh Muse: "Manifest"
Fine Madness: "Empire," "Life and Death at the DMV"
Green Mountains Review: "Barley"
Indiana Review: "Good Morning"
Lilliput Review: "Heaviness"
Literal Latte: "Grammar"
Maverick Magazine: "Ardor," "Pastoral," "Prayer for Safe Travel,"
        "Zap"
The New Hampshire Review: "Satellites"
No Tell Motel: "$500,000 Policy," "And Then," "If I Had Another
        Face," "My Sentimental Education," "Shanty"
The Ohio Review: "Afterlife," "Declarative"
Quarterly West: "Gulf Coast"
River City: "Story Problems"
Salt Hill: "Every Step a Trespass"
Slant: "Prayer Against Dying on Camera"
Softblow: "Scenes"
Tampa Review: "Alias"
Tattoo Highway: "Winter"
Three Candles: "God's Job," "Poem for a Public Bus Placard,"
        "Stricken"
Yellow Silk: "Augury"

I am indebted to Greg Kosmicki and The Backwaters Press for publishing this book, Deana Riddle for her cover design, Gail and Teresa for their keen proofreading, and to Philip Levine for selecting the manuscript.

For their friendship, encouragement, and criticism, many thanks to Joel Brouwer, Jim Ciletti, Lois Hayna, Jane Hilberry, David Keplinger, Jenn Koiter, Rebecca Laroche, Malcolm McCollum, Carol Morrison, Matt Schumacher, Jane Wampler, and Jake Adam York.

ABOUT THE POET

Aaron Anstett received his M.F.A. from the Iowa Writers' Workshop, where he held a Teaching-Writing Fellowship. Later, he was the Halls Poetry Fellow at the Wisconsin Institute for Creative Writing at UW-Madison. His first collection, *Sustenance,* was published by New Rivers Press in 1997. Recently he has taught creative writing at Colorado State University-Pueblo. He lives in southern Colorado with his wife and children.